Musical Mystery Tour

fun songs for children from 4 to 104

HILARY JAMES & SIMON MAYOR

©1992 by Hilary James & Simon Mayor
First published in 1992 by Faber Music Ltd
3 Queen Square London WC1N 3AU
All songs by Hilary James & Simon Mayor except for
'The fat fat farmer' by Andy Baum & Simon Mayor
'I like to eat' trad., additional words James/Mayor/Baum
'Wait for the wagon' trad., additional words James/Mayor
Cover and all illustrations by Hilary James
©1992 by Hilary James
Music processed by Silverfen
Printed in England by Reflex Litho Ltd
All rights reserved

ISBN 0 571 51324 7

by way of a preface...

These songs were all written for children,
But grannies and grandads will do.
Even teachers have sometimes joined in, and we hope
That whoever you are, so will you.

You'll find choruses typed in *italic*,
And barlines to help you with scan.
But when singing calypsos remember the trick
Is to fit as many words into one line as you possibly can.

Be ready to gobble like turkeys,
Or squawk like a parrot indeed!
And listen to cautionary tales of a king
Who fell foul of gargantuan greed.

There are flocks of flamingoes and fresh fried fish fillets
To give you a well twisted twongue.
You can have a quick blast at singing it fast
But you'll probably get the words wrong!

Chords for guitarists are written on top,
With 'undifficult' parts for piano,
But make of these songs whatever you will
In your own individual manner.*

Use a recorder, a 'glock' or a drum,
Or whatever else might come to hand.
Remember a saucepan that's played with a 'feel'
Sounds as good as a Yamaha Grand...**

There are songs that we hope make you giggle,
And others that might make you think.
And we know when you've done singing 'I like to eat'
You'll be gagging for something to drink.

You may like to add some new verses
About eating or jungles or humming,
But the finest advice we can possibly give is
Keep singing, keep banging, keep strumming.

*　*This verse rhymes in Sheffield!*
**　*'Steinway' didn't scan!*

Hilary & Simon.

contents

Hilary James and Simon Mayor have written and performed songs for radio and television, on programmes ranging from *Play School* to *Newsnight*. Their 'Musical Mystery Tour' show has entertained both adults and children in schools, theatres and festivals from Orkney to the Channel Islands and as far afield as Singapore.

'Musical Mystery Tour' cassettes and CDs

These songs and many more can be found on the 'Musical Mystery Tour' series of cassettes and CDs which feature a wide range of instruments, some surprising sounds and zany sketches! For details of these and live performances by Hilary James and Simon Mayor contact:

Acoustics Records
PO Box 350
Reading RG6 2DQ
England

Christmas
The snowman's song　4
I like to eat　8
When the snow falls softly down　9
Gobble gobble gobble gobble gobble!　20
The story of the Australian Father Christmas　26

In the jungle
Hum hum hum　6
I love all the fruit　22
The parrot song　24

Down on the farm
The fat fat farmer　7
The farmyard tango　18
The donkey can-can　19

Tongue twisters
Sleepy sheep　10
A flock of fat flamingoes　12
Will a willow　32

Travel
Up in a big balloon　14
Wait for the wagon　16
Clickety clack　17
My bike　23
The road to Banbury　31

Recycling
A magpie sitting on a broken chair　28
King Wastelot and the right royal rubbish dump　30

3. There was once a snowman climber
   who climbed up a snowy peak,
   But he didn't feel like climbing down
   'cause his legs had got too weak.
   But snowmen they are clever,
   in the mountains you can spot 'em;
   They turn into an avalanche
   and slide down on their bottom!
   It's c c c c cold (etc.)

4. | Pity the poor | snowman
   | out in a Winter's storm.
   An old top hat and a football scarf
   are all that keep him warm.
   He'd sooner sit inside the house
   by the fireside nice and snug,
   But if he did he'd turn into
   a wet patch on the rug.
   It's c c c c cold (etc.)

During the chorus rub your hands together, shiver your shoulders, show with your hands how a chimp's teeth chatter, raise your teacup, then do some more hand rubbing and shivering.

Hum hum hum

2. Tell me monkey, if you know
   How the words to my song go.
   "Chatter," said the monkey,
      "Chatter, chatter, chatter.
   I don't think the words
      to your song matter."
         Hum, hum, hum, (etc.)

3. Tell me crocodile, if you know
   How the words to my song go.
   "Snap!" said the crocodile,
      "Snap! Snap! Snap!
   If you don't know the words
      you can clap, clap, clap."
         Hum, hum, hum, (etc.)

4. Tell me goldfish, if you know
   How the words to my song go.
   "Bubble," said the goldfish,
      "Bubble, bubble, bubble.
   Don't sing the words,
      it's too much trouble."
         Hum, hum, hum, (etc.)

5. Tell me wise owl, if you know
   How the words to my song go.
   "Well," said the wise owl, "Don't be glum,
   The words to your song go,
      'Hum, hum, hum.' "
         Hum, hum, hum, (etc.)

This song came from a joke. "Why do humming birds hum?" "Because they don't know the words." How many jokes do you know? Start your own joke book and make up some of your own if you can.

The fat fat farmer

2. For lunch he has a rabbit pie
   and a shepherd's pie and a cottage pie,
   With gravy and peas and extra meat
   and beer, and now he's sat on my seat!
   Timothy Tractor is my name (etc.)

3. For dinner he has chicken and chips
   and pizza and chips, and fish and chips,
   And strawberry yoghurt
      and Christmas pud
   with cream, and now I'm
      stuck in the mud!
   Timothy Tractor is my name (etc.)

I like to eat

3. I | always order rice with curried chicken
   When fish is steaming I can hardly wait,
   I'm also fond of jellied eels and frog's legs
   And if I'm | really starved
      I sometimes eat my plate.
      I like to eat (etc.)

4. | I like cheese from lots of
      different countries
   I | keep it in a great big plastic box
   I | leave it for a month or
      sometimes longer
   'Cause then it smells just
      like my sweaty socks!
      I like to eat (etc.)

5. Last year I started guzzling at the trifle,
   Intending not to leave a single trace.
   My brother came and said
      that I was greedy,
   So I | picked it up and
      pushed it in his face.
      I like to eat (etc.)

Brightly

I like to eat, (I like to eat) I like to eat, (I like to eat) and no mat-ter what it is I like to eat. I like to eat.

1. I like to swim and fish and mo-del rail-ways
2. I love ap-ples me-lons and ba-na-nas;

Or go-ing out at night to hunt a ghost. But more than all of these I'm fond of eat-ing,
Chest-nuts are quite nice with-out the skin, But more than all of these I love an o-range,

And Christ-mas is the time I eat the most.
Es-pe-cially when the juice runs down my chin.

When the snow falls softly down

1. When the snow falls softly down we're happy as can be, For we like playing in the snow but others disagree. The poor old duck on the ice is stuck, "Quack! Quack! Quack! Quack!" The rusty old train must stop again, "Chuff! Chuff! Chuff! Chuff!" Our old car won't get very far, "Peep! Peep! Peep! Peep!" But what of Santa on our rooves, his reindeer sliding on their hooves? I hope that they can pull the sleigh to bring our toys on Christmas Day.

2. In the snowy weather we like to run and play, Making snowballs, digging deep, and riding on our sleigh, but...

Try adding sound effects during the chorus. You may like to do the sounds just with your mouth, but an old cycle horn would do for the car and some music shops sell duck calls and train whistles.

—9—

3. I was | walking through the woods
　　when the wind began to whistle,
　So I wore a woollen woolly but
　　I caught it on a thistle.
　I tore my woollen woolly and
　　I couldn't make it better
　So I sheared myself a shaggy
　　sheep to knit another sweater.
　　　*It's not surprising
　　　sheep are sleepy, (etc.)*

4. I | knit a woolly sweater and
　　| then I did some more,
　And | in the end I had a pile of
　　jumpers on the floor.
　| One was red with big blue spots,
　　and one was pink and green,
　The biggest brightest woolly
　　jumpers I had ever seen.
　　　*It's not surprising
　　　sheep are sleepy, (etc.)*

A flock of fat flamingoes

Like a Cossack folk song
(steadily at first, speed up gradually)

2. A flock of fat flamingoes
   had eaten all they could,
   And when they tried to fly away
   they sank down in the mud.
   There they lay all Saturday,
   and through 'til Sunday morning,
   When a crocodile gave the flock a smile
   and ate them without warning.
   *Fresh fried fillets
   of fresh fried fish (etc.)*

3. A flock of fat flamingoes
   began to fight and kick
   Inside the friendly crocodile
   who then was promptly sick.
   As one by one they left his tum,
   and spread their wings in flight
   They dreamt of fillets of fresh fried fish
   and their feast next Friday night.
   *Fresh fried fillets
   of fresh fried fish (etc.)*

This song gets gradually faster all the way through. See how fast you can get without stumbling over the words. Try making up your own twongue tisters – I mean ting twosters. You know what I mean!

Big balloons fly because they are filled with a gas called helium, which is lighter than air.

* No chorus between verses 2 and 3, and 4 and 5.

Wait for the wagon

2. The Queen goes to the theatre
　　in a gleaming black Rolls Royce.
　She'd sooner ride a wagon,
　　but queens don't get much choice.
　So she | waits until her holidays
　　to do her favourite things,
　And then she rides a wagon
　　and this is what she sings:
　　　Wait for the wagon, (etc.)

3. | Buses go to Bristol,
　　trains to London town
　But we | can't go far in our old car
　　'cause it's | always breaking down.
　So the | only way to travel
　　in sunshine or in snow,
　Is a ricketty racketty wagon
　　and we'll sing as we go:
　　　Wait for the wagon, (etc.)

4. I've got a poor old donkey
　　with great big floppy ears,
　His legs are rather wonkey,
　　and they | have been many years.
　We go out every morning
　　and he | pulls my wagon along,
　And | as he goes HEE! HAW! HEE! HAW!
　　HEE! HAWlways sings this song:
　　　Wait for the wagon, (etc.)

Clickety clack

Moving along

1. Clickety clack, clickety clack, the rickety train comes down the track.
   Clickety clack, clickety clack, the rickety train is coming back.
   Do you know who is coming today, is coming today?
   Do you know who is coming to stay, is coming to stay?
   Clickety clack,...

2. See the world go flickering by
   Past hedges and fields and clouds and sky.
   Flickering trees and telegraph poles,
   The rickety train just rattles and rolls.
   Do you know who (etc.)

3. Under a tunnel and over a hill,
   The rickety train is rattling still.
   Hear it whistling far away
   Along the coast and round the bay.
   Do you know who (etc.)

Percussion idea:

* or similar

The rhythm of this song sounds like a train trundling along the track. Some can whisper "Clickety clack" very quietly in rhythm while others sing the words. Can you hear which part of the tune sounds like a train whistle?

* Small notes: optional descant

The farmyard tango

2. There was a cow whose
    charms were entrancing,
   She met a bull who
    took her BULLroom dancing.
   He said "Come | closer and
    I'll show you how it | goes."
   But she | fainted when he
    trod on all her | toes.
     Down on the farm (etc.)

3. There was a horse who
    suffered from hay fever,
   She kept on sneezing, and
    nothing would relieve her.
   When she | tangoed some hay
    got up her | nose,
   So she | sneezed and dribbled
    on her | toes.
     Down on the farm (etc.)

4. There was a drake who
    had some good luck,
   He had a dance with a beautiful duck,
   He | kissed her with great
    big slobbery | smackers,
   And he | whispered, "You
    drive me | quackers!"
     Down on the farm (etc.)

5. There was a pig with a
    rather pretty nose,
   Who took up ballet and
    balanced on his toes,
   But des|pite all his
    elegance and | grace,
   His nose is | flat,
    'cause he landed on his | face.
     Down on the farm (etc.)

Percussion idea:

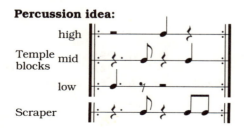

The donkey can-can

One day a | donkey tried to do the can-can
just to prove he could-could
kick his legs as high as anybody else,
But sadly he danced a little madly
and kicked a passing bee,
who stung him on the knee.

As he hopped about the floor
   the bee went buzzing through the door,
So he danced a little more
   and soon the sweat began to pour.
He didn't know what was in store,
   his knee was stung and his feet were sore,
Furthermore he swore and swore
   he'd no more dance the can-can.

Poor old donkey!

Hee! Haw! Hee! Haw!

And so the | donkey tried to do the can-can
just to prove he could-could
but he couldn't 'cause he quickly lost his breath
And so he started a new dance-dance,
it was called the "can't-can't"
but it's not as good!

Sung to the well-known tune of the 'Can-can' by the French composer Jacques Offenbach. This was a popular dance about 100 years ago. It involved kicking your legs high in the air, and wasn't very graceful! How high can you kick your legs? Have you made up any crazy dances lately?

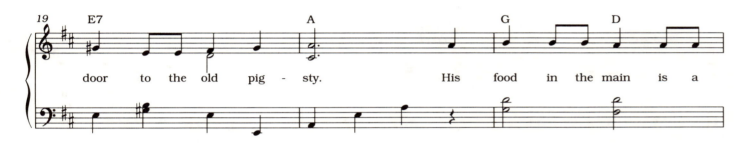
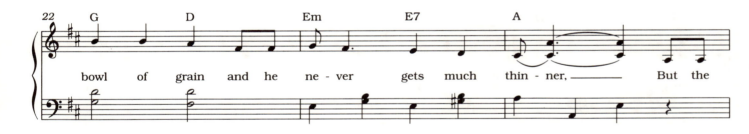

2. A | turkey and a duck got married one day
    in the | summer when the
        bright sun | shone.
    The | hens and geese made up the choir
    and the | vicar was a goat
        with a | dog collar on.
    The duck declared her life-long love
    and the turkey did not squabble,
    But when he came to recite his vows,
    he | just said, "Gobble! Gobble! Gobble!"
        Gobble gobble gobble gobble gobble! (etc.)

3. | Thomas the turkey bought a car
    that | never went anywhere,
    'Cause the | steering wheel was in the boot
    and all four tyres were square.
    The headlights pointed up to the stars
    and the engine was no good,
    So he pushed his feet
        through the holes in the floor
    and he peddled as fast as he could.
        Gobble gobble gobble gobble gobble! (etc.)

4. | Thomas the turkey couldn't fly
    so he | built a flying machine.
    The wings were made of an old bedsheet
    and he | sat in a bucket in be|tween.
    With his upper lip stiff, he jumped off a cliff,
    | Oh! what a terrible drop!
    Then he wobbled like jelly and
        he landed on his belly
    and he bounced right back to the top.
        Gobble gobble gobble gobble gobble! (etc.)

This song has got some crazy actions. Try them as you sing the chorus: gobble with your elbows, run and fly with your arms, wobble your whole body, and finally gobble with your elbows again.

I love all the fruit

3. Tarzan looks for banana
    to make banana milk shake,
    He uses | forty bananas;
    now Tarzan's got tummy-ache.
        I love all the fruit (etc.)

4. Tarzan swings from the creepers,
    he swings all over the place,
    And when he swings into | pineapple tree
    he gets a very flat face.
        I love all the fruit (etc.)

5. Tarzan drives through the jungle
    in a rusty old car,
    And when he bangs into
        | angry rhinocerous
    he goes "Aaaaagh! Aaaaagh! Aaaaagh!"*
        I love all the fruit (etc.)

6. Tarzan likes to go paddling,
    he paddles more than he oughta.
    And when he paddles in | crocodile river
    his legs end up shorter.
        I love all the fruit (etc.)

* *Do your best Tarzan yodel*

You can make jungle drums using saucepans and tins, scrapers from sand paper blocks. Make animal noises with your voice. Monkeys chatter, lions and tigers roar, elephants trumpet, parrots squawk ... and Tarzan yodels!

My bike

With a calypso swing

2. I | took up roller skating,
    it | seemed a simple sport.
   It looked so quick and easy,
    or at | least that's what I | thought.
   But using brakes on roller skates
    is difficult to master
   And | I woke up in | hospital
    with both my legs in plaster.
   On my bike (etc.)

3. And when I took up jogging,
    my heart was really thumping,
   Un|til I reached a river bank
    and had to practice jumping.
   I knew it would be easy,
    of this I had no doubt,
   But I | missed it by a million miles
    and squashed a passing trout.
   On my bike (etc.)

4. So | some day you might see me,
    riding by on my bike.
   | I don't care what's good for me,
    I'll just do as I like.
   And so I'll stick to cycling,
    'cause that's my biggest thrill.
   It's easier than any sport,
    especially going downhill.
   On my bike (etc.)

Percussion idea:

The parrot song

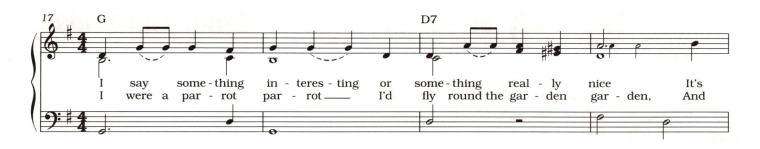
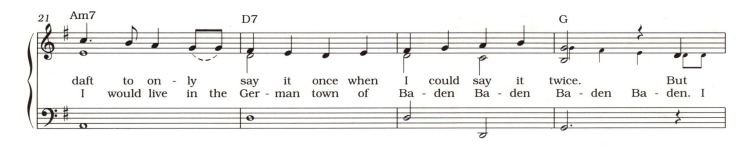

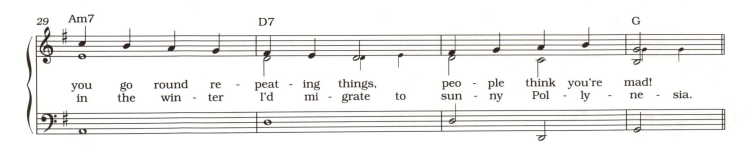

3. If | I were a parrot policeman
   I | wouldn't say "Hello".
   I'd | say "Hello! Hello!
     Hello! Hello! Hello! Hello!"
   And | if I joined the army
     | wouldn't it be super
   I | couldn't join the Royal Marines,
     I'd | be a parrot-trooper.
     I'm a parrot (etc.)

4. If | I were a parrot-parrot
     I'd | live in Hong-Hong-Kong-Kong.
   | I'd play tennis, I'd play tennis,
     and | also ping-ping-pong-pong.
   Yes | I'd repeat-repeat things so soon
     | everyone would know,
   That the | art of saying things just once
     is dead as a dodo-dodo.
     I'm a parrot (etc.)

Although parrots talk, they never learn many words and have to repeat the same few over and over. Remember to put on your best parrot voice for "Pieces of eight! Pieces of eight! Who's a pretty boy?"

The story of the Australian Father Christmas

2. Now Santa set off round
  Australia in the setting sun
  He hoped to visit every town
  before the night was done.
  But reindeer's hooves are made for snow
  and not for desert sand
  And things weren't moving quite as fast
  as Santa Claus had planned.
  And as he sat and scratched his head
  and wondered what to do
  Some funny looking animals
  came hopping into view,
  "Kangaroos!" He cried aloud,
  "I'll hitch them to my sleigh,
  And I'll | travel round Australia
  in a most Australian way."
   *It's a sunny, sunny Christmas
   in Australia (etc.)*

3. Now Santa's sack was tightly packed,
  | just like tinned sardines
  And all the presents tumbled out
  as it split round all the seams.
  He | hadn't got a | needle,
  he | hadn't any cotton
  And the spare he normally took along
  he'd bloomin' well forgotten.
  | "Can I be of any help?"
  said the biggest kangaroo
  "If you've | nowhere else to | put 'em
  per|haps my pouch will do."
  The others offered likewise,
  and before the break of day
  He'd called at every house from
  Alice Springs to Botany Bay.
   *It's a sunny, sunny Christmas
   in Australia (etc.)*

Because Australia is on the other side of the world, their seasons are reversed, so Christmas is usually hot and sunny.

A magpie sitting on a broken chair

2. The small birds rise and
    take to the wing
   and think of their nests to be
    built in the spring.
   No-one to see them, no-one to care
   but a magpie sitting on a broken chair.

   And the magpie's song
    soon reaches the ears
   of the people in the town,
    but nobody hears.
   No-one to listen, no-one to care
   but a magpie sitting on a broken chair.
       And the magpie sings (etc.)

3. But if we listen, | if we care
    for the magpie's song
   and the birds of the air,
   We can | use all the things
    that we threw to the breeze;
   | save our hills and the lonely trees.
       And the magpie sings (etc.)

This song was written originally for SCRAP (Sheffield Community Recycling Action Programme). Magpies have a reputation for collecting all sorts of things that we throw away. It may be rubbish to us, but to them it's real treasure.

—28—

King Wastelot and the right royal rubbish dump

Now once upon a shooting star beyond the Dingley Dell
There was a king called Wastelot who lived right royal well.
He loved to spend his money and went shopping every day,
And as he kept on buying new he threw the old away.

One day he threw away his crown and thought it was fantastic
To buy a new one every day in different coloured plastic!
He hated dirty cars but never let his servants wash 'em,
He simply sent them down the tip for a big machine to squash 'em.

He was fond of woolly jumpers, but he never wore them twice.
He had a new one every day no matter what the price.
The sheep were not too keen to meet this regular delivery
'Cause every one was sheared and shorn and ended up right shivery.

He used his chairs and tables for a bonfire every night
And bought a set of new ones every day with great delight.
He used a silver knife and fork, a china plate and cup
And smashed them after dinner 'cause he hated washing up.

But when his sheep ran out of wool the king was not too pleased;
He'd no more wood for furniture 'cause he'd chopped down all the trees.
He couldn't find a knife and fork or plate to hold his dinner,
So Wastelot, the wealthy king, began to grow much thinner.

What happened to those plates and cups, his jumpers and his crown?
What happened to the brand new cars that drove around the town?
He'd thrown them all away, of course, the silly royal chump!
And now the only thing he had was a great big rubbish dump.

But now the story moves on to the king who lived next door;
King Savelot used everything a thousand times or more.
He even saved his rubbish up in great big bins and then
He sent it to his factories to use it all again.

And Wastelot who'd long admired his palace, gave a sigh,
"I used to buy nice things," he said, "when there were things to buy."
King Savelot just smiled a smile, and waved his royal hand,
"You may have owned this once," he said, "I got it secondhand."

This poem about a wasteful king could form the basis of a play. Try making up your own music and sound effects for Wastelot and Savelot (pronounced "Waste-a-lot" and "Save-a-lot").

The road to Banbury

2. And when the apples began to fall,
when the apples began to fall,
I saw five hundred stars in all
on the road to Banbury.
   Fishes may swim (etc.)

3. And one of the stars fell out of the sky,
one of the stars fell out of the sky,
So I held out my hand as it twinkled by
on the road to Banbury.
   Fishes may swim (etc.)

4. And then the star became a spring,
then the star became a spring
With seven young salmon
   a-learning to sing
on the road to Banbury.
   Fishes may swim (etc.)

5. And one of the salmon's as big as I,
one of the salmon's as big as I,
Now do you think I am telling a lie
on the road to Banbury?
   Fishes may swim (etc.)

6. One of the salmon's as big as an elf,
one of the salmon's as big as an elf,
If you | want any more more you can
   sing it yourself
on the road to Banbury.
   Fishes may swim (etc.)

These very mysterious words were based on an old English folk song. We changed a couple of verses and added a chorus and a new tune.

Will a willow

2. I asked a shady character
    if he could shed some light
  On why a weeping willow tree
    might weep all through the night.
  He said to ask a neighbour,
    a fine upstanding sort,
  And so I knocked upon an oak
    and asked him what he thought.
  And then I heard the pining
    of some pine trees in the wood.
  I asked if they could help me
    and they said perhaps they could.
  They knew the weeping willow,
    he often felt so sad,
  But once he'd had a real good cry
    things never seemed so bad.

3. Will a willow wilt
    or will a willow won't?
  Why do weeping willows weep
    when pussy willows don't?
  Would a wood of willows
    wail and whine and weep?
  Or would a wood of weeping willows
    cry themselves to sleep?
  Once a willow washes,
    and once it dries its eyes,
  It looks down at the water
    and it has a nice surprise;
  Another weeping willow,
    a cheerful friendly tree,
  Smiling at the weeping willow
    keeps him company.

The tune to this song sounds oriental, and is made up of the notes D E F# A and B. If you play a musical instrument, you can make up your own oriental-sounding tune by playing around with these notes. You can get a similar effect by using just the black notes on a piano.

— 32 —